Why Does Lightning Strike?

by Megan Cooley Peterson

Bullfrog Books

Ideas for Parents and Teachers

Bullfrog Books let children practice reading informational text at the earliest reading levels. Repetition, familiar words, and photo labels support early readers.

Before Reading
- Discuss the cover photo. What does it tell them?
- Look at the picture glossary together. Read and discuss the words.

Read the Book
- "Walk" through the book and look at the photos. Let the child ask questions. Point out the photo labels.
- Read the book to the child, or have him or her read independently.

After Reading
- Prompt the child to think more. Ask: Have you ever seen lightning? Did you know it is electricity? What more would you like to learn about lightning?

Bullfrog Books are published by Jump!
5357 Penn Avenue South
Minneapolis, MN 55419
www.jumplibrary.com

Library of Congress Cataloging-in-Publication Data

Names: Peterson, Megan Cooley, author.
Title: Why does lightning strike? / by Megan Cooley Peterson.
Description: Minneapolis, MN: Jump!, Inc., [2024]
Series: Science questions | Includes index.
Audience: Ages 5–8
Identifiers: LCCN 2022049671 (print)
LCCN 2022049672 (ebook)
ISBN 9798885244909 (hardcover)
ISBN 9798885244916 (paperback)
ISBN 9798885244923 (ebook)
Subjects: LCSH: Lightning—Juvenile literature.
Classification: LCC QC966.5 .P495 2024 (print)
LCC QC966.5 (ebook)
DDC 551.56/32—dc23/eng20230117
LC record available at https://lccn.loc.gov/2022049671
LC ebook record available at https://lccn.loc.gov/2022049672

Editor: Jenna Gleisner
Designer: Emma Almgren-Bersie

Photo Credits: Reeva/Shutterstock, cover; mishooo/iStock, 1; PhilipYb Studio/Shutterstock, 3; Cary Meltzer/Shutterstock, 4; Pau Buera/Shutterstock, 5; Filip Drevojanek/Shutterstock, 6–7 (clouds); kritskaya/Shutterstock, 6–7 (ice crystals); Jirat Sarmkasat/Shutterstock, 6–7 (waterdrops); Polonio Video/Shutterstock, 8–9, 23tr; Bartosz Lewandowski/Dreamstime, 10–11, 23bl; mdesigner125/iStock, 12–13, 23bm; Cultura Creative RF/Alamy, 14–15, 23tl; Meindert van der Haven/iStock, 16; smikeymikey1/Shutterstock, 17; MangoStar_Studio/iStock, 18; Frank L Junior/Shutterstock, 18–19, 23br; Cavan Images/SuperStock, 20–21 (girl); Phatthanit/Shutterstock, 20–21 (sky), 23tm; Luisa Leal Photography/Shutterstock, 24.

Printed in the United States of America at Corporate Graphics in North Mankato, Minnesota.

Table of Contents

White Light

The wind blows. Rain falls from storm clouds.

Lightning strikes.
Why?
Let's find out!

lightning

Clouds have waterdrops.

They have bits of ice, too.

ice crystals

clouds

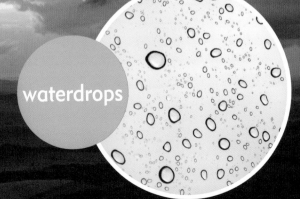

waterdrops

positive charges

negative charges

8

The waterdrops and ice bump into each other.

This makes charges.

The charges jump back and forth.

It makes electricity.

It makes lightning!

Lightning looks white.
It jumps to other clouds.

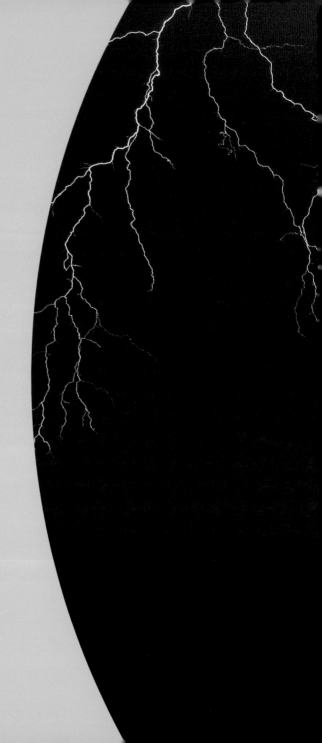

Zap!

Lightning strikes.

It travels to
the ground.

Why?

negative
charges

positive
charges

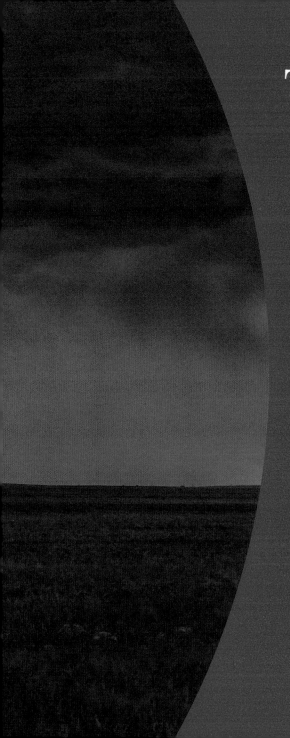

The ground has charges, too.

It pulls the cloud's charges.

Lightning is hot.

It zaps a tree.

It can start a fire.

17

Lightning warms the air.

The air gets bigger.

It happens really fast!

Boom!

We hear thunder.

The storm ends.
The sky clears.
Let's play!

How Lightning Strikes

Electricity builds up inside storm clouds. It creates lightning. How does lightning strike? Take a look!

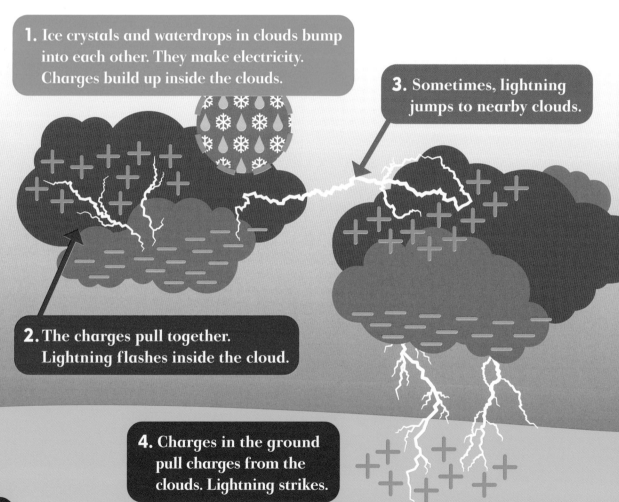

1. Ice crystals and waterdrops in clouds bump into each other. They make electricity. Charges build up inside the clouds.

2. The charges pull together. Lightning flashes inside the cloud.

3. Sometimes, lightning jumps to nearby clouds.

4. Charges in the ground pull charges from the clouds. Lightning strikes.

Picture Glossary

charges
Positive and negative electric particles.

clears
Becomes bright.

electricity
A form of energy caused by moving particles.

lightning
Flashes of light when electricity moves between clouds and the ground.

strikes
Hits suddenly and with force.

thunder
The loud sound that comes during a storm after a flash of lightning.

Index

To Learn More

Finding more information is as easy as 1, 2, 3.

❶ Go to www.factsurfer.com

❷ Enter "whydoeslightningstrike" into the search box.

❸ Choose your book to see a list of websites.